Homes around the world

Mountain Homes

Nicola Barber

Crabtree Publishing Company
www.crabtreebooks.com

Crabtree Publishing Company
www.crabtreebooks.com

Editors: Hayley Leach, Ellen Rodger, Michael Hodge
Senior Design Manager: Rosamund Saunders
Designer: Elaine Wilkinson
Geography consultant: Ruth Jenkins

Photo credits: Danita Delimont/Alamy p. 24; Robert Harding Picture Library Ltd/Alamy p. 16; Craig Lovell/Eagle Visions Photography/Alamy p. 10, p. 27; Suzanne Long /Alamy p. 13; Malcolm Park/Alamy p. 18; George Philipas/Alamy p. 20; Profimedia.CZ s.r.o./Alamy cover and p. 7; Stockfolio/Alamy p. 14; J Marshall-Tribaleye Images/Alamy p. 8; TNT Magazine/Alamy p. 23; Andrew Watson/Alamy p. 15; Wilmar Photography.com /Alamy p. 9; Jan Butchofsky-Houser/Corbis p. 12; Epa/Corbis p. 19; Christian Veron/Reuters/Corbis p. 17; Walter Bibikow/Getty Images title page, p. 11, p. 26; Paula Bronstein/Getty Images p. 6; Michael Melford/National Geographic/Getty p. 25; Keren Su/Lonely Planet Images/Getty p. 22; Greg Epperson/Photolibrary p. 21.

Cover: A mountain home in the Himalaya Mountains in Asia.

Title page: People have carved out homes in these volcanic rock formations in Cappadocia, Turkey.

Activity & illustrations: Shakespeare Squared pp. 28, 29.

Because of the nature of the Internet, it is possible that some website addresses (URLs) included in this book may have changed, or sites may have changed or closed down since publication. While the author and publisher regret any inconvenience this may cause the readers, no responsibility for any such changes can be accepted by either the author or the publisher.

Library and Archives Canada Cataloguing in Publication

Barber, Nicola
    Mountain homes / Nicola Barber.

(Homes around the world)
Includes index.
ISBN 978-0-7787-3545-8 (bound).--ISBN 978-0-7787-3557-1 (pbk.)

    1. Mountain people--Dwellings--Juvenile literature. 2. Dwellings--Juvenile literature. I. Title. II. Series: Barber, Nicola. Homes around the world.

GN392.B37 2007   j392.3'609143   C2007-904709-2

Library of Congress Cataloging-in-Publication Data

Barber, Nicola.
  Mountain homes / Nicola Barber.
    p. cm.
  Includes index.
  ISBN-13: 978-0-7787-3545-8 (rlb)
  ISBN-10: 0-7787-3545-1 (rlb)
  ISBN-13: 978-0-7787-3557-1 (pb)
  ISBN-10: 0-7787-3557-5 (pb)
  1. Dwellings--Juvenile literature. 2. Mountain people--Dwellings. I. Title.

GT172.B375 2008
392.3'6--dc22   2007030184

Crabtree Publishing Company
www.crabtreebooks.com   1-800-387-7650

Published in Canada
Crabtree Publishing
616 Welland Ave.
St. Catharines, Ontario
L2M 5V6

Published in the United States
Crabtree Publishing
PMB16A
350 Fifth Ave., Suite 3308
New York, NY 10118

Published by CRABTREE PUBLISHING COMPANY
Copyright © **2008**

Contents

Words in **bold** can be found in the glossary on page 30

What is a mountain home?

A mountain is an area of land that is much higher than the land around it is. Many mountains have **steep**, rocky sides, which are often covered with snow.

▲ This mountain village is high in the Himalayas.

Mountain life
The highest mountain in the world is Mount Everest in the **Himalayas**.

There are mountains all over the world. Many of them are in large groups called **mountain ranges**. Many people have homes in the mountains.

▲ *This house stands alone, high in the mountains.*

Towns and villages

Some people live in large towns and cities that lie in **valleys** high in the mountains. Others live in small villages, or in houses on mountain slopes.

◀ The city of La Paz, Bolivia, is built high in the Andes mountains of South America.

The steep slopes of mountain ranges can make it difficult to travel through mountain areas. People who have homes in the mountains often live far away from other people and places.

▲ *This mountain home, in the European Alps mountain range, is called a "chalet".*

Hot and cold places

Some people live in mountain areas that are very cold and wet. They build their mountain homes with steep roofs so that the rain and snow will slide off easily.

▼ *Old mountain homes in Japan have steep roofs made from straw.*

Some mountain homes are in places that are hot and dry. These pointed rocks are in Cappadocia, Turkey. People have **carved** out the rock to make houses to live in.

▲ *You can see the windows of the homes in the rocks.*

Building a mountain home

It is difficult to transport **materials** across the mountains, so people often build their homes from the materials that they find nearby. In some places, the mountain slopes are covered with thick forests. People cut logs from the trees to build their homes.

▼ *This mountain home is being built out of logs. It is called a "log cabin".*

In other places, there are few trees, but there is plenty of stone and dirt. People build their houses from stone, or from **bricks** made from mud.

▲ *These houses are in a mountain town in Ethiopia, in Africa.*

13

Inside a mountain home

This home is high in the mountains of the French Alps. The thick walls of the house keep the inside warm, even when there is snow and ice outside.

▼ *The furniture in this kitchen is made from wood.*

This woman lives in a house made
out of stone in the Atlas Mountains of
north Africa. She keeps cows and sheep.
Her animals live in part of her home.

▲ The house
has a flat roof
made from wood
and grass.

The weather

The weather can change very quickly in the mountains. People who live in the mountains can expect sunshine, rain, wind and snow — all in one day! During the winter, most mountains have a lot of snow.

Mountain life

Special chains are put on car tires to stop wheels from slipping on the snow.

▲ *Snow covers a small village in the French Alps.*

In the spring and summer, the snow melts. The water from the melted snow fills mountain streams and rivers. Many mountains also get a lot of rain. When the ground gets very wet, it sometimes slides down the mountain. This is called a **landslide**.

▲ A landslide destroyed homes in this mountain village in Venezuela, South America.

The environment

Mountains can be dangerous places to live. **Avalanches** are one of the biggest dangers. An avalanche happens when large amounts of snow slide down steep mountainsides. On steep mountain slopes, **barriers** are used to try to stop avalanches from burying villages below.

▼ *These barriers will slow the speed of avalanches by stopping the snow.*

Sometimes there are **earthquakes** in mountain areas. The shaking of the ground makes some houses fall down. It is often difficult to reach people in mountain areas after an earthquake.

Mountain life

A huge earthquake in 2005 destroyed homes in the Himalayas in Pakistan and India.

▲ A powerful earthquake in India destroyed this woman's house in 2005.

19

School and play

In mountain areas where there are not many people, school classes may have only a few students. It can be difficult to find teachers who want to work high up in the mountains. Some children travel to schools in larger towns nearby.

▼ *These students are in class at a mountain school in Bolivia, in the South American Andes mountains.*

Living in the mountains can be fun!
In the winter, children learn to ski down
the mountain slopes and skate on frozen
lakes. People go walking in the mountains
in the summer, when the snow has melted.

◀ Mountain biking
is a popular activity
in the summer in
the lower levels of
some mountains.

Going to work

Many people who live in the mountains are farmers. Mountain farmers grow crops and **graze** animals such as **yaks**, goats, and sheep on high **pastures**. In some places, farmers have cut wide steps, called **terraces**, into the mountainside to make flat areas to grow their crops.

▼ *People grow rice on this terraced mountainside in Long Ji, China.*

In the winter, **tourists** come to the mountains on vacation. People who live in the mountains sometimes work in restaurants and shops in ski **resorts**. Some also teach tourists how to ski.

Mountain life
The highest ski resort in the world is Chacaltaya in Bolivia, in the Andes. Chacaltaya means "cold bones"!

▲ Chair lifts carry skiers up the mountainside in the Alps, in Austria.

Getting around

In some places, there are no roads to high mountain villages. People must walk along paths called **trails** to reach their homes. They use animals, such as yaks and **llamas**, to carry their goods on the trails.

▼ *This yak is carrying goods up a trail in the Himalayas in Nepal.*

◀ *This train is taking goods through the Rocky mountains in Western Canada.*

Mountain roads and railways zigzag up and down steep slopes. In winter, deep snow may close high mountain roads. In many places, there are long tunnels, so cars and trains can go through the middles of mountains.

25

Where in the world?

Some of the places mentioned in this book have been labeled here.

Look at these two pictures carefully.

- How are the homes different from each other?

- What is each home made of?

- Look at their walls, roofs, windows, and doors.

- How are these homes different from where you live?

- How are they the same?

Cappadocia, Turkey

ROCKIES

NORTH
AMERICA

PYRENEES

ATLANTIC
OCEAN

PACIFIC
OCEAN

ANDES

SOUTH
AMERICA

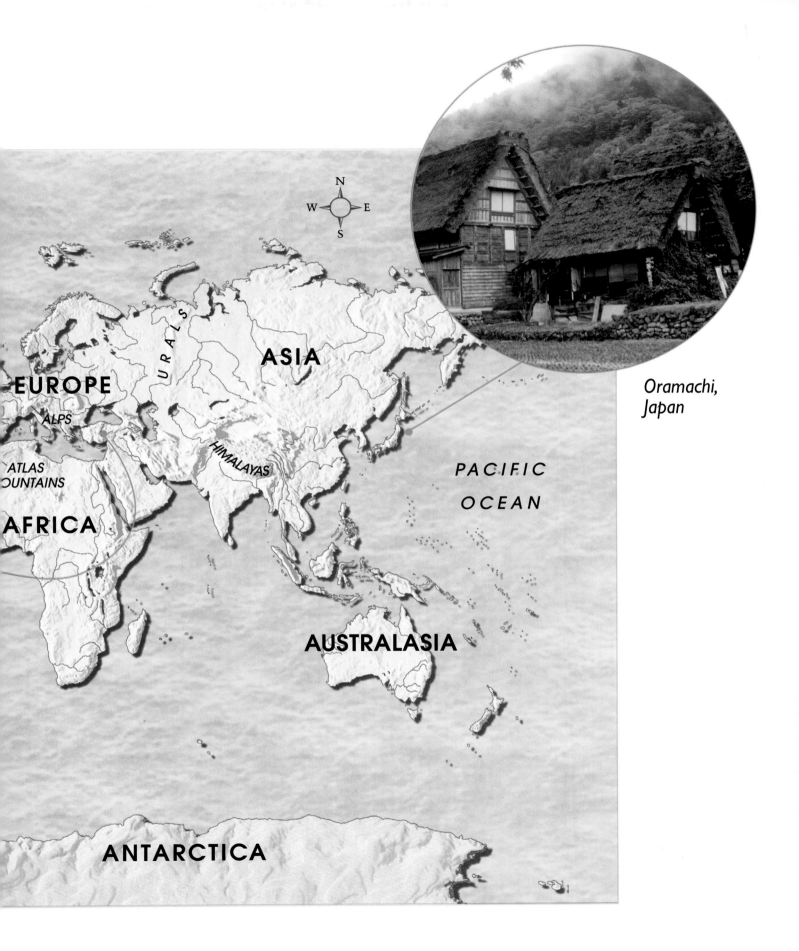

EUROPE

ASIA

AFRICA

ATLAS
MOUNTAINS

ALPS

URALS

HIMALAYAS

N
W   E
S

PACIFIC
OCEAN

AUSTRALASIA

ANTARCTICA

*Oramachi,
Japan*

To the top of the mountain

Play this mountain game with a partner.

What you need
- paper
- sticky notes
- pencil
- crayons
- scissors

---

1. Cut three small squares from a piece of paper. Make game cards by coloring one square blue, one red, and one yellow.

2. Put the cards in a pile with the colored side facing down.

3. Make your own game piece by cutting a small square from a sticky note. Make sure that there is adhesive on the back of your square. Write your initials on your square. Each player must make a game piece.

4. Use page 29 as your game board. Place the game pieces on the START square. Choose a game card. Move your game piece to the next colored square that matches the color on the card. Then answer the question written on that square. Use this book to see if you answered correctly. If so, take another turn. If not, it is your partner's turn. The person who gets to the last square on the board first, and answers the last question correctly, wins!

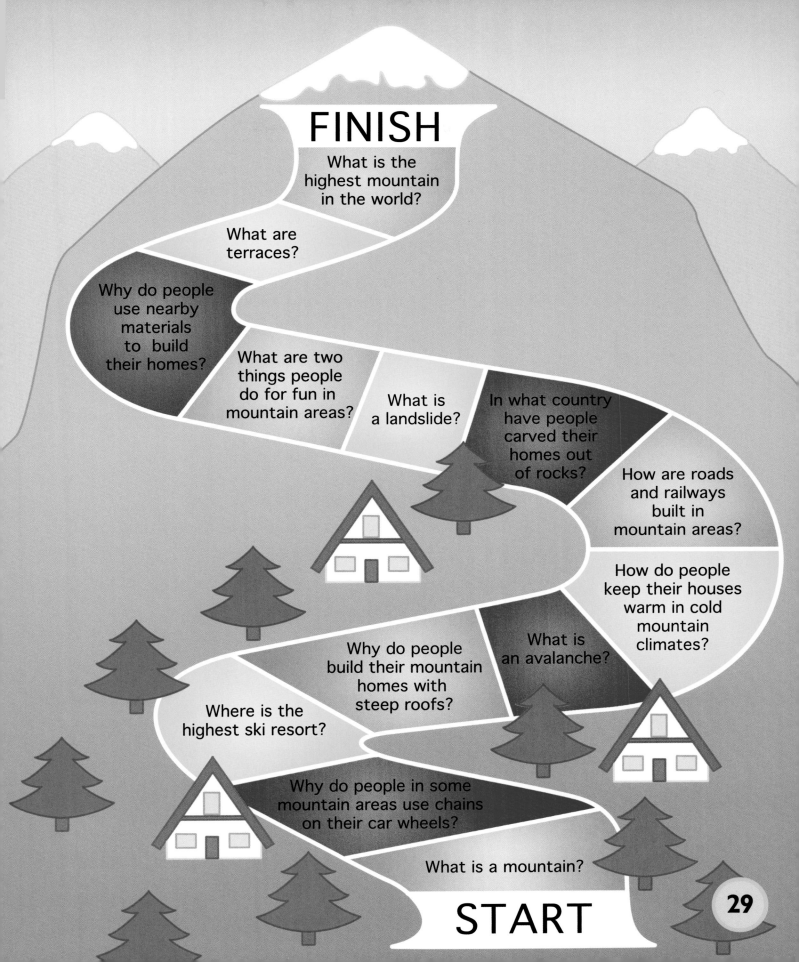

FINISH

What is the highest mountain in the world?

What are terraces?

Why do people use nearby materials to build their homes?

What are two things people do for fun in mountain areas?

What is a landslide?

In what country have people carved their homes out of rocks?

How are roads and railways built in mountain areas?

How do people keep their houses warm in cold mountain climates?

What is an avalanche?

Why do people build their mountain homes with steep roofs?

Where is the highest ski resort?

Why do people in some mountain areas use chains on their car wheels?

What is a mountain?

START

29

Glossary

avalanche	When huge amounts of snow slide down a mountainside
barrier	An object that stops something from getting past it
brick	A hard block of mud and sand that is used for building
carve	To cut away
earthquake	When the ground moves and shakes
graze	To eat grass
Himalayas	A huge and very high mountain range in South Asia
llama	An animal from South America that is used to carry goods. People also use its fine hair to make clothing
material	What something is made of
mountain range	A group of mountains
mudslide	When mud and water slide down a slope
pasture	Land covered with grass where animals go to graze
resort	A place where people go on vacation
steep	A steep slope is one that rises very sharply
terrace	A flat area of ground
tourist	A person who is on vacation in a place
trail	A path or track
valley	A low area of ground surrounded by higher areas
yak	A hairy cattle-like animal that lives in the mountains of central Asia

Further information

Books to read

Mountains and Deserts, from the Nature Unfolds series
Illustrated World Atlas
Pakistan, from the Land, Peoples, and Cultures series
Life in Ancient South America, from the Peoples of the Ancient World series
Mountains, from the Wonders of our World series

Websites

http://www.mountainvoices.org
First-hand interviews with people who live in the mountains

http://www.brocku.ca/geography/people/dbutz/shimshal.html
The Shimshal Nature Trust of Pakistan, a mountain community's plea to protect their land

http://www.mountain.org/education/explore.htmx
An online resource about mountains

http://www.mountain.org/
The Mountain Institute website

http://www.4learning.co.uk/essentials/geography/units/mount_bi.shtml
Geography site

http://www.mountainpartnership.org/issues/issues.asp
Mountain Partnership website

Index

All of the numbers in **bold** refer to photographs.